The Footing

The Footing

Angelina Ayers
James Caruth
Mark Goodwin
Rob Hindle
Andrew Hirst
Chris Jones
Fay Musselwhite

Longbarrow Press

Published in 2013 by
Longbarrow Press
76 Holme Lane
Sheffield
S6 4JW

www.longbarrowpress.com

Printed by T.J. International Ltd,
Padstow, Cornwall

Poems © Angelina Ayers, James Caruth,
Mark Goodwin, Rob Hindle, Andrew Hirst,
Chris Jones, Fay Musselwhite 2013

Editorial, introduction and design © Brian Lewis 2013

Jacket photograph © Nikki Clayton 2013

The poems featured in this anthology are previously unpublished,
with the following exceptions: Angelina Ayers, 'Ball Street Bridge' and
'Stone Walls and Snowgates' (*Iota 92*); James Caruth, 'Close of Play'
and 'Procession' (*The Sheffield Anthology*); Rob Hindle, 'Princess Street
to the Wicker' (*The Sheffield Anthology*); Fay Musselwhite, 'Path Kill'
and 'Impasse' (*Matter 9*), 'Boulder' (*Matter 10*).
Thanks to the editors concerned.

ISBN 978-1-906175-21-4

First edition

Contents

Introduction

'Every walker is a guard on patrol to protect the ineffable.'
Rebecca Solnit, *Wanderlust: A History of Walking*

The roots of this anthology were seeded by two slender pamphlets that appeared from Longbarrow Press in 2008. The first of these, James Caruth's *Dark Peak*, is a long poem in the form of a Catholic Mass, set in an area of the Peak District that lies a few miles west of the city of Sheffield. The second, Matthew Clegg's *Edgelands* (republished in Clegg's Longbarrow collection *West North East*), is a sequence of poems that offers a different route out of the city, mapping the hinterland of industrial estates, housing developments and common land that broadens and blurs its northern edge. Both of these works can be read as 'walking poems', but neither of them foregrounds the *act* of walking; the mode, like the route, is inferred gradually, step by step.

The poems in *The Footing* are the result of a long-term engagement with the ideas and practices of walking; an engagement that, in many cases, starts at home. As 'home' for six of these seven poets is Sheffield (Leicestershire-based Mark Goodwin being the exception), it is perhaps unsurprising that much of the ground covered in this anthology should fall within its boundaries. While the focus of the poems is often local, however, the outlook is never parochial. Familiar ways are made unfamiliar by acts of attention to hitherto unseen details. Landscapes are disturbed and reordered by the currents of memory and history. Path and place are shadowed by loss, and become contingent and uncertain. There are, too, sustained flights of imagination, in which migratory routes are reconstructed from traces and rumours, footsore iconoclasts strip churches of their pictures and ornaments, and domestic rooms are displaced by riverine boulders. The common thread running through the anthology is the idea that Rebecca Solnit attributes to the great walking poet William Wordsworth: that of walking as 'a mode not of travelling, but of being', a process that involves the mind and the body.

We enter *The Footing* through the parish of Stannington, a village on the north-western edge of Sheffield that lends its name to the first poem in James Caruth's *Tithes*, and exit in the wake of a destructive raid on the city centre: the last, eastward movement of Rob Hindle's *Flights and Traverses*, a sequence of five one-way journeys spanning the period 1782-1940. The poems that lie between (and beyond) these points also find new and unexpected ways to 'lay the margins down': Chris Jones' *Death and the Gallant*, which reimagines the Reformation as a path of slow, conflicted destruction; Angelina Ayers' *The Strait*, where the walls and weirs of the River Don provide shelter for elegy and quiet surprise; Mark Goodwin's coastal epic *From a St Juliot to Beyond a Beeny*, shortened and reshaped for this collection; Fay Musselwhite's *Breach*, which paces the banks of another Sheffield river (the Rivelin), a site of retreat and renewal, congestion and flux; and *Three Night Walks*, Andrew Hirst's meditation on regret and remembrance.

While the poems in this anthology are attentive to the legacies of conflict and loss – both public and personal – that shape our experience of the landscape, they are also alive to the possible worlds that are envisioned, if only briefly, in the act of walking; the paths behind us, and the paths before us.

Brian Lewis

Tithes

James Caruth

Stannington

Twenty-five years a foot-soldier,
pensioned to this high scrape
of heather and bracken.

Build stone walls
against the slow march of hills.

Pace out the acreage:
Nethergate, Uppergate, Knoll.

High Riggs

No, this is the cruellest month.
January, the old year passed on,
the sky over High Neb
emptied of light.

From off the valley a wind
edged with ice
stirs the couch grass,
the earth is pungent with the dead,

my head suddenly full of voices
and faces I can't put a name to.
I sit down by a grey-green wall
to watch a dog sniff a trail by the hedge,

both of us slipped the leash, searching
these borders for a scent of home.

Memorial

He pauses here most afternoons,
adjusts the weathered wreaths.
He won't stay long, just time enough
to count a tithe of names he knows by heart.
Then home to catch the evening news,
one more coffin's slow parade
from the belly of a transport plane.
He puts the teapot down,
and another day ends in Helmand
as two young men kick the desert
from their boots, stare at a camera lens
and think of home as a village like this.
Outside evening settles in the trees,
the street lights come on one by one.

Quaker Grave
Bowcroft Cemetery

Hardly room to bend a knee
in this cramped space
God fills with silence.
The parish cast you out,
this broken stone their testament.

You died, it says, in the fifth month.
Now again, this May morning
is lit by low sun as a breeze
carries woodsmoke up from the farms.
My head's humming, I'm strung out
like the power lines bordering the valley

wondering why I'm drawn
to this famished field,
by some uncorroborated memory of home
where great quarrels were born
over such small issues.

But here there is no dispute,
this strip of hill holds all of you.
These exiled bones claim a world
from one small square of earth.

Closed Order

Someone said, across the valley
there is a closed religious order,
a community of nuns whose days
are filled with contemplation.
A wordless congregation
that shuts out the world.

Today, the heather is burning
on Bradfield Moor, white smoke
drifts low against a perfect sky.
By Kirk Edge a breeze shivers the grass
all down the endless fields. Tell me,
what faith abandons this.

How is it God is found in such absences;
when lovers will drive out here at evening
to watch the stars undress, as a million miles
stretch out between here and there.
Their whispered love set free
on a journey that seems beyond us all.

Close of Play

On the empty terrace of the Rose & Crown
geraniums drip from baskets, red petals
and glasses scattered on the tables
as a summer's day draws to a close.

The front page of a discarded newspaper
flaps open on a picture of young faces
in desert fatigues, blank eyes staring
below headlines of zones, and new offensives.

Beyond the lane a derelict field
of untended grass runs down to tangled
boundaries of bindweed and nettle.
If I was half a poet, I would imagine

a bowler running in, hear the *tock*
of ball on bat, see lithe ghosts
throw down their caps to chase hope
all the way to a white picket fence.

The rustle of a breeze in the ash trees
might be the opening of applause.
Across the valley clouds are gathering,
thunder breaks miles away and somewhere
an umpire offers the light.

Parish

We lay the margins down
among our first words:
tree, mountain, river.

While here on the city's western edge
the stump cross marks a beginning
as a late summer sky falls open
and light encloses us.

Some say this was once sea-bed
and if we dig deep enough we would gather up
small finds of shells, stone memories of kelp.

So now the land's insatiable for rain,
the ancient weight of water.

On days like these, I take into myself
something of the earth below my feet,
give this place whatever name I have for home.

I walk the boundaries,
pace out a language I will know it by:
chrann, sliabh, abhainn.

chrann   tree
sliabh   mountain
abhainn   river

Procession

For fifteen minutes I have been going nowhere,
while rain falls through the overhanging trees,
rattling like stones on the bonnet of my car
as a herd of cows moves from pasture to byre.
On the edge of the city, life passes in slow procession.

Big as boats, their hides are white oceans,
lapping black continents. The great hips
swaying in ponderous rhythm, pink udders
full to bursting. They pause to pull grass
from the ditch, with tongues thick as my arm.

At the rear, two herdsmen in clabbered boots,
flat caps pulled down over faces shiny as apples,
slap at the stragglers with salley sticks, waving
their arms as they read the sky over Lodge Moor.
Somewhere, important events are taking place.

But on this narrow lane a herd of Friesians,
impassive eyes like pools of black water,
make a journey they have always made,
and evening settles to the pulse of a car engine,
fingers drumming on a steering wheel.

A Stone

I leave this stone here on top.
You will not feel its weight
but maybe somehow know the touch of it.

Like a thrush's egg,
worn in the mouth of the stream
that turns along the valley floor.

Grey shale, as the sky
paling to evening.
A piece of these soft hills

where we carve out
our own small space.
A stone I'll leave in memory of that.

Nocturne

Two lights blink in the night sky,
a plane on descent to Manchester
may see a faint glow in the darkness,

houses on a hillside barely defined
by a scattering of lights. Within each one
a TV set purring in blue contentment,

while dreams go to seed in posturepedic beds,
to blossom like dark tulips in the early hours
as a cat on a backyard fence cries to the moon.

Night settles over everything, over cars
heading home along the lanes, over
the lost boys draining a can of lager

outside the single row of shuttered shops.
2.00am, deserted avenues and cul-de-sacs
are a street light run for a dog-fox

searching in the half-closed bins.
The breath of clipped lawns
mists in the chill air.

A town hall clock chimes the hour.

Death and the Gallant
Chris Jones

for Susan Hatton

XXIII. Also, that they shall take away, utterly extinct, and destroy all shrines, coverings of shrines, all tables, candlesticks, trindals, and rolls of wax, pictures, paintings, and all other monuments of feigned miracles, pilgrimages, idolatry, and superstition, so that there remain no memory of the same in walls, glass windows, or elsewhere within their churches and houses; preserving nevertheless, or repairing both the walls and glass windows; and they shall exhort all their parishioners to do the like within their several houses.

From *The Royal Injunctions of 1559*

26. UFFORD, JAN. the 27th. We brake down 30 superstitious Pictures; and gave direction to take down 37 more; and 40 Cherubims to be taken down of Wood; and the chancel levelled. There was a Picture of Christ on the Cross, and God the Father above it; and left 37 superstitious Pictures to be taken down; and took up 6 superstitious Inscriptions in Brass.

27. WOODBRIDGE, JAN. the 27th. We took down 2 superstitious Inscriptions in Brass; and gave order to take down 30 superstitious Pictures.

28. KESGRAVE, JAN. the 27th. We took down 6 superstitious Pictures; and gave order to take down 18 Cherubims, and to levell the Chancel.

29. RUSHMERE, JAN. the 27th. We brake down the Pictures of the 7 deadly Sins, and the Holy Lamb with a Cross about it; and 15 other superstitious Pictures.

30. CHATSHAM, JAN. the 29th. Nothing to be done.

31. WASHBROOK, JAN. the 29th. I broke down 26 superstitious Pictures; and gave order to take down a stoening Cross and the Chancel to be levelled.

From *The Journal of William Dowsing, of Stratford*
(Demolishing the Superstitious Pictures and Ornaments of Churches within the County of Suffolk, in the Years 1643-1644)

I *The Adoration of the Magi*

Drove road to Saint Botolph's; psalms of wind
sound the tree-tops. None to meet us
when we wade the flooded meadows of the parish,
then come dripping through the orchard.
Brown hangs his boots and shirt about the porch.
We have a scout. Here are four wooden crosses,
stones that whisper *Ora pro nobis*,
star-breasted angels, and high above a northern arch

slow Magi loom from out the night.
Jasper's fit for fields more than a palace;
he kneels with gold that flares like tips of wheat,
his bare head touched by sun, grace, solace.
I fetch a ladder. Brown works the whitewash,
and just for good measure, cuts Mary's face.

II *A Reckoning*

I doze through storms in a godly farmer's barn
while Brown lies coddled in his mistress's bed.
I shouldn't bemoan my hard and dusty stead
but when Brown crows in the grey light of dawn
More haste, old man, I've ached less of mornings.
A seven-mile trudge under skies of lead
toward a spire craning high above the woods
like a heron eyeing a poppled stream.

More reckoning – swift effacement and flames –
as if what's blighted can be razed outright
and yet my wife is fourteen years a shade,
my five children I hold to my left-hand side
though to give each girl a name and age
would mean to clear the long grass from the grave.

III *The Crucifixion*

Saint Anne's. The Passion on a southern wall.
When Nicodemus hefts his body down
this artist shows by Christ's pulled arms
the frame is slight yet burden's all.
As Brown stirs water into pails of chalk
I trail my shadow round this Lord's demesne –
closed cottages, forge, tavern, farm –
to root out screens made scarce and shrouded panels.

I've dug up roods like briars from a ditch,
once found a Christopher standing in a yard.
Doused in this wheat-ears' ruby light
I absolve my eyes from searching hard.
I turn a bottle's murky shine, then lift
it high to pledge my disregard.

IV *The Doom or Last Judgment*

Solemn over this chancel arch the Doom.
On this side, Peter lifts an arm to collect
a swim of souls, like silver from a net.
Beneath, the dead clamber from narrow tombs.
I point at sinister and say to Brown
there's ones like you, stewing in sex…
But Hell's not prised for Brown's gathered elect.
And you, old man, do you rise or go down?

Snow falls on fire. Saved and damned lie buried
under snow. Christ and his colours
under drifts of snow. A frost will crust this nave
for stone years, bone years, well-deep years.
Now that Brown's gained a horse he'll bolt ahead
while I ruminate under the shattered stars.

V *Saint James the Great*

Brown won't abide it but we're pilgrims too.
James, brass-limbed, bestride a transept wall
bears a low-slung pouch, yellow scallop shell,
his outstretched staff a warship's prow.
Brown the supplicant, could he bend so low,
would hear the North Atlantic's swell
against those flame-rigged citadels
and whisper prayers to this *Matamoros*.

He knows I see him check his hand
so has me daub out heraldry,
the face, the heart, then holy land.
Noon-wise, I find him supine under trees
clasping tied-up inventories and plans
like a sullen knight in effigy.

VI *The Tree of Jesse*

More rain to fill the butts and troughs
as gargoyles spew forth sermons on the flood.
While Brown turns stables out for buried goods
I scale the Jesse tree before it's cut
and keep an aerie in its ample boughs.
A priest's dragged in with cries about a rood,
Brown's right arm tight around his head.
He's moved against the stone-carved font

and this man's christened with streams of blood,
a veil of crimson down his goggling face.
Now Brown will haul him from the muddy road
to the recusant Lord's estate
so that he might be understood.
This will teach us to hide our faith.

VII *The Last Supper*

Are you drunk again, old man?
Look up I say, *none want for wine but Judas,*
but Brown no longer sees the pictures.
Slacken from work and I'll mark your skin.
So flesh too is made a painting
where one reads things base or superstitious,
my wrist a cut from being dangerous.
Brown would brand me among the damned.

Here's forty strokes to flay a painter's hand,
strike comely flesh back into chalk-white bone.
Christ's little nest of fingers won't withstand
the guest who's given silver and breaks his home.
His eyes, his azure eyes I blind,
his skin I mark outright, and so I'm done.

VIII *Death and the Gallant*

I wake thick dust as chapel-sunlight pales
and into silence lift my stubborn breath.
Here's a courtier touched by wanton Death:
look how Thin-Bones jigs along the aisle,
fingers teasing up a dusky rose.
For our dandy turned by this address
how ill-judged his hat and boots and lacy cuffs
since he'll be fucked by a smirking corpse.

Brown has spies along these ferny roads.
I know he wants me dancing from a rope.
I will inter my sketchbook and my beads,
stow what bread I can procure about my coat,
and pick a trail over these moonlit fields.
What ghost disturbs my dark but my old love.

IX *Spirits*

The woods are free with spirits, faeries, elves:
they moth my thoughts now dawn makes light of me.
I bless my boots to find such company
plagued as sprites are to bide amongst themselves
in dank and dappled corners of the realm.
Look how few they have become, how airy
under oak sway, waning almost to memory.
We listen. For miles downwind the clamour of bells.

Brown lies close in some burgher's dainty house,
a knife and Bible set beside his bed.
Blessed the man who wakens to a chorus,
to panes of green and gold on a stream's rapt flood;
hails sky's thick blossom on high-domed boughs
even if his gentle friends have flown or fled.

X *A Reckoning*

Best fight your wars on boggy fields.
As Brown halloos me by a brimming ditch
I come out carrying a hefty stick
to walk secure, to have a block to wield.
Brown moves like fire through the blighted wheat
but when he swings his blade the hot-head slips.
I stand, pivot, meet him with a kick
then club about his body and close-cropped head.

No pardon or last words: I cut him good.
He knows the journey of his immortal soul.
I drag then bury him deep inside the wood
and push a branch to crest the mud-filled hole.
I've breath enough to make my peace with God
then pray that Brown be delivered from hell.

The Strait
Angelina Ayers

The Bench

On these moss-wet slats
a stranger's name is carved above the inscription
One touch of nature makes
the whole world kin.

                   My remembering's
a bus across town, so I sit here, borrow
someone else's dead.
                 What do they think
when they think about you,
and this perishable view everywhere –

leaves everywhere
                   bracken and oak
like broken bones on the bluish path,
turtle-green tapers scorched to brass, spirals
of snuffed candle smoke –
                 others keep their fire
blood orange-red and glowing
          as though lit from inside.

I snatch sight of you, stranger,
flame of blue-tipped bird skulking
                   the underbrush,
thistled between glances.

           You crouch in my unhatted head
with your trowel and samples, a mote
of sloughed-off skin in my eye
               making me

name the breed of an egg
by its weight in my hand, the Latin
                         for all these leaves.
          I conjure you
from falling flecks of image and dust –
             the black cloud of your hair fills
the sky to a storm, as if you're up there and not
          hands and knees in the earth.

Ball Street Bridge

Past the cutlers, halfway over the Don
I stop to watch the river's dull pewter
slow-shimmy the strait, grinding stone,
cutting shingle. Mallards perch the weir

sloped in water-gush and slugs of rain
like dregs of Kelham Ale. I envy their grit,
webbed roots dug down against the braid
of ore-heavy stream, a quiet unshifting.

With moonrise, light pivots as it fails.
The suds beneath glint with gudgeon
and coltsfoot smoulders the watery soil,
yellows the banks like fire. I want to learn

this knack of standing still while headwaters,
washing past, whittle rocks to quartz.

Off Derek Dooley Way

(A snicket down to the Don –
beyond the Wicker's pizza bar
and late night pharmacy,
fluorescent-strip-lit pill bottles,

luxury-model mobility scooters –
a yellow wagtail grubbing
in the tipped up crack willow,
margherita box greaseproof lining

and empty twenty Benson.
We walk Cobweb Bridge, back
and to, suspended with the echo,
and the wagtail trips from silt

to overgrowth, no Fruit Shoot
or blister pack unturned. Wild figs
bulge bruise-black, their leaves
reflecting in the old water.

Knotweed creeps through
scrapyards, and solder-hot air
cools over salmon runs.
Isn't that we met here enough?)

In the soft grey summer mizzle
we set out for the five weirs
having lived here thirty-odd years
and yet to make it to the end.

Stone Walls and Snowgates

An angler wades in   teetering like a goose
slips on loose silt
                      churned by the Don.
Water rushes past and round him   hip high
        November cold.

The crack willow's ready to tip.
Browning catkins loom on the water.
White geese play in its shallow roots

far from the furnace
         the fire and soot.
                          Only the splash
of red-brick rubble   a broken bumper
                        stuck in the rushes
lets slip the road, the way this river
burst its banks after rain, reached up
        to these stone walls and snowgates
and had a good look at the streets
laced grey with industry   sloped home
with sewage
              and steel dust in its stomach.

He baits his hook and casts to the current
      waits for barbel to bite
in the echo of the gas bell
    the ore-brown walls of Tommy Wards
      the tinny crash of the weir.

from *From a St Juliot*
to Beyond a Beeny

being just some of the metres
taken from a longer walk

Mark Goodwin

from Kilometre One

(at metre one)

... tree-foliage coils
like green froth
across a St Juliot

Church, stone
feelers of finials poke
up from breeze-
vibrated leaf-spray

a giant snail waits
for a her & a me

to our left or north

a slope of coppery-
green-barley-sheen each
wind-touched
ear conveys
waves of sense
tive tremblings a
watery flow of
crop in chaos pran
sing & trickling like lit
flood lapping at
our thighs as
we walk a
hedge path

at slope-top a hedge-crest
where wind-bent hawthorns curl
like surf

above us

so my friend I love & a me are below
slant-lit green

at a bottom of a field

we are under
neath

summer's growth for us floods a
Lea-on-Ness

whilst a St Juliot's snail feels sky

we neath
summer's
lea whilst

from Kilometre Two

a Valency widens
and our path now touches
its banks as
a Minster Wood full
of tall bible-barked
but sappy parishioners holds
swathes of leaf-pale
underlight fractured
and dotted by
brown shadows

we step down
from a bank path
onto slate shelves
river water has
bevelled

slate's dry grey
& wet blue-dark
& silvered water-lit edges

& seen noise, solidified
to clear liquidity obeying
gravity's imperative
& water's will
of circles, flows
like nothing spoken
for a first time forever

an undulating sheen
of crystalline yet
gelatinous light
slides & rolls tight

chaos over
layered pages
of still slate

& each little slate
-lipped abyss
seen or unseen
in this river slips
its location slips
its placeness slips

through 'imagine'

walking on
paper part

from Kilometre Three

we walk on

on paper
contours part
as a valley-bottom
begins to broaden
our boots chlink
on slate-scree
coppice-clumps
of young hazels
sprout from this
metallic-chipped
& glinting ground
thistle gorse heather
purples & yolk-yellows
sun-inflated fragrance
presses our skins
and we talk of water
released from sky
to moor then shed
to be constrained
by ground's narrow
grooves accelerated thrust
to a boiling
brown liquid plough
vicious & fast passing
to rip at trees here
& people's houses down
river

a blackbird's
wet notes now
deepen space

    blackbird's now space
    on mass glints colours

from Kilometre Four

surf
can just be heard
as we walk towards
a Pen Ally Point
a narrow harbour below
rippling gently as fresh
Valency meets salt
soft glugs & sloshes against
carved slate blocks
two stubby buffer-piers
like pin-ball flippers form
a kind of valve between
calm human harbour &
utterly careless sea

SW095914
Boscastle Harbour

    soft carved two
    like a calm utterly

45

from Kilometre Five

I chew a sprig of samphire
aromatic hot & salt grows
in my mouth like a ghost
or momentarily compressed ocean
then fades to tint
my saliva

salt-greased wind slicks
our cheeks and
rattles our clothes

and to west seagulls shattering
their wet-glass voices over
a hogsback rock of a Mea Chard
or May Shard like a slate
ship capsized
or huge Unterseeboot
rising

then far
beyond this fragment of land an ocean-curve
of a planet's horizon

and my friend
I love has found
in a crack in slate

a plump woodlouse-like creature
segmented & grey as its slate realm

far curve horizon friend

from Kilometre Six

distance shows sheen

& shade
liquidly repeating
tumbles like unseen
people &
creatures she

is counting
her seals below
seven in sea's
swirls of o
ther world she
is shot through
with animal as
each

dark doggy
head or mer
maidish body

resolves in surf

see she
sheen sheer

she shry
soaked shrines

eyes rise she
shines she sure

and a taste
of plum I'm
eating now
glows rouge
in my mouth

in my mouth
a fruit from
a living plant and

a part of world

mouth from & world through

she sure taste

from Kilometre Seven

we agree how easy
it is to miss
a way

how hidden
abysses have
trivial lids
how our steps cross
over nothing

we kiss and we   we our a
're on our

                    o

way a

path of slate-shards traverses
wide convex slopes
of monotone
beige-grassed heath

we've entered
a suspended
expanse of rounded
ground cut

off by coastal-curve
behind & before
us & above
slope-curve fades
to sky & below

SW105922
heading north
then north east

I know unseen
cliffs plunge only felt
as slight thuds of
sea-crash
or at least

an I & we & you
can imagine
we feel that

we follow a filament balanced

between sky
& sea we are

specks like alpinists
on a high altitude snowfield
sea's vast vertigo a
horizontal of vertical
our tiny figures

are condensed space
we are distance
we are distances
distance is us

we are only seen

by sky's
& sea's

too wide
blue eyes

from Kilometre Eight

I buckle
down to working
up gradient here
now and be
gin enjoying
rhythm & mountain
memories of
movement

for a moment
I'm my mum
on a Lakeland
fell's steep ridge
I see her eyes
frightened but
focused like
light between
clouds she is
meek & unsure
of mountains but will
not give in &
is vivid with glad
ness as long as
I stay close
and hold
her hand on
broken ground

steep slate steps
switchback

glad as close hold on ground

from Kilometre Nine

not far now
we cross

boggy ground
badly poached
by cattle

we're surrounded
by tall prehistoric plants
like giant cow-keck
this is where a Bee
Ny stream springs
from to run some
two kilometres only
to plunge as a Pent
Argon Falls

we step over
a thin string
of stream onto
firmer ground

an orchestra of
wind-conducted
grass-heads rubs
against our trousers
it's like wading
through dry liquid
waves breaking lit
seed-foam over
our boots

now suddenly two huge sleek
      conker-brown horses canter

                                              waves seed our now

Breach
Fay Musselwhite

Boulder

Only by bringing it home
could she get its measure.

How this was done
she doesn't remember.

She must have been drunk.
Now her favourite hunk of millstone grit

pulled from the river's bed
vested in moss and white oxalis

has swallowed the room
land-grabbed most of the carpet.

Her children inch round this cuckoo's egg,
listen to floorboards starting to give.

Contra Flow

Coaxing a skank of hair
from a slow plug hole,
I'm back
ankle deep
on the Rivelin bank,
stick in hand ripped
from a mown down tree.
We're tunnelling
under a low stone bridge
through a pileup
of crashed wood re-routed
by flash floods,
freeing the bottleneck
of leaves and rocks
and bits of twig,
thrilled at the flicker
of a ripple when
a trickle licks a passage
filtering its pressure-load,
a goit to ride high
while the main drag races
down the weir.
Clear for a moment under stone –
stuck in the silted throat
and hard to swallow,
we tug, cajole
a sand-filled traffic cone
flushed down from the road.

Path Kill

After several days,
between outcrops of fur
and its silvery moss remains,
a pouch, bin-bag black,
creases at the underbelly
like a baby's wrist,
still foetal, kidney shaped,
held from dew and rain.

Woodlouse and fly families later,
flat stacked in fraying layers
dog-eared rug-matted black
leaf-like in leaves, secret
in bramble and buttercup,
ransacked, leaching back.

Impasse

The bone in her heart grows up past her throat
crackles its chill in her
                        stone cold cheek

she can't talk it away so she walks it
down by the river's raw bite.

She stalks the rimy bank of a tongue
for where water will wear away bone
each footstep following one of her own.

On shale, under blear, limestone chains
lie like spines in the shallow gravel bed.

Snagged in rock at a weir's head, a dog-leg
of thorn-rusted twig, hoar-coated

in feathers like bleached iron filings, clings
to robin-red hips hard-glazed
                           in the current's breath.

Now the blood's in her belly

the sleet in her chest hacks up, grist
to her grind, spits out over her lip's crust.

Spume crests the bitter flow
                     melt swells.

By the lee path she leaves riven depths, treks
through woods' winter skeletons, broaches the burn

to the ice field, stone still.

Three Night Walks
Andrew Hirst

I.

They say I'm a poet of the city
– the simplest of things, a night fish flung out
from the drought, acute angled orange.
I'm on my way back from somewhere to somewhere else
back past the floodlit stadium, unsettled, absent, scouring
quickened gestures, harnessed songs.
They say I've forgotten who I am, who any of us are
– that horrible little woman from *Gwent News*
the gossip settling against a methadone coloured sky,
down a rough hillside among the shell cases and thorns
of gorse, that at night we dream of meadows.

One version of it, set sharp after twenty years
– it happens to be raining on Alferston St.
on Monaghan Rd. and Mayes Rd., the cars stand still.
Two boys, just kids, want my money. But I want my money
more and for the first time I'm not easily letting go.
So I stare them out, close in on one of the faces like a camera.
It's enough to scare them off. I'm lucky.
Lucky I don't see the two kids again in every unsettled face
nor look for semaphore to change the young
– stuff to force blame into – mosque, backstreet or purse string.

I'm lowly, coarse, my dark brow sweats.
Yes, I'm a city poet, I adore rain on asphalt, the abandoned Moses
basket in the bushes, music and light bristle from every pore.
But it's night times mostly now, scuttling along the curb's ledge
alone, unsettled, residual, the lights from a passing car
news of a niece's love slowed down, twenty years set sharp
– blood caked feet, dim lit wall, forecourt
– as when you first awoke, two drops of water on a bow
pearline glass, opalescence, coal.

II.

All my life I wasn't sure if I believed in poetry
– running down the Kingsway, at seventeen, free,
lido on the left, painted blue, the smell of the empty sea
nerves talked black and good tidy houses
to the right, houses I lived in, believed from.
Toward the evening, the salt trees
become whiter, effervescent, every day's end the same
thought, insects, new hatched, stuck to the pool's surface
– at sixteen, seventeen, an empty gesture.

Same thing, years later, Bounds Green in large white rain
the only time I loved the mornings – smell of geraniums
books against a borrowed window, smell of the markets
filling up to the right, marking every move
– one thing or another always becoming broken.
I had more then, my life was filling up, I was keen to taste
a little of everything and felt in an unfettered moment all
of that learning to be leading somewhere, worth something.

Amongst the few mementos that I kept
were two letters written in the early sixties
from my own mother to my father before they were married.
She was nineteen and there was a charm to them
that I expressly repeated to myself
over and over, their naivety pure, untarnished.
I showed them no one else and hid them away after
my own love failed. I married early, because of love
and because I was told from an early age to always marry
upwards, I always tried to fit to what others wanted
– an empty gesture later I became ashamed of.

III.

The last street lamp at last far behind me
a carbon lump of land rises and dips, the residue
from a fable, although more tentative now.
This is the one I knew when we went back late
and caught the icy moon between bare branches
napping on the still lake, the blue black
of Pascal, thick breath clouds out, who threw his hands
over his last candle to silence it, a child's tremulous murmur.

As I approach still further down the road
an old ewe, whose patch this truly is, bellows out a warning
– there's no quietness here or anywhere tonight.
In deficit, the thin contemporary distance flattens
unfamiliar names on dry tombstones, a white alarm beckons.
I'm drawn to it just as I am to water
– the sound keeps me alive.

As if still in wet ink, I suddenly remember
those beautiful lines from St. John of the Cross
– *There he stayed sleeping and I caressed him*
and the fanning of the cedars made a breeze
And then right at the end the bit about being sedated by lilies
– I follow the moorland curvature until
residual light blooms over in the next valley beyond.
I don't know where I am nor where
any of this is leading, but feeling my way over
the density or lightness of things I do not have
to think of memory very much
of foxhole, shattered meadow, oak's bare branches.

As the late bus home pulls down onto empty outskirts
I again begin to draw the future from memory
– at *Hope Wakes* I watched a girl winched down
onto a white mare all the male villagers swished
with oak fronds as a symbol of renewed virility.
I don't know if it works in reverse but within the year
my best friend became glacial and moved away.
We never spoke again but through photographs
– our marooned, irregular faces full of coyness.

Flights and Traverses
5 Itineraries
Rob Hindle

Grindleford Bridge to Fulwood, October 1782

The supposed migration of Richard Marsden, an ancestor.

A day of sun and old green,
your face dim in the river.
Behind, a dog shifts in the lane,
snuffs your trodden earth
and slumps on the muck.

The road curves and lifts to the rock-line.

Somewhere behind the toll house
a bird clamours at a cat
or stoat
out
out
I watch your name dry,
hear the pennies counted in.

October.
Everything sounds against a silence,
is measured against its end.
Crows dwindle in the pale air;
the barn shows its ribs, their shadows
long on the grass, frail.

Where are you going?
Far as I can.
When will you get there?
Evening.
Where have you come from?

Over the moor.
Will you return?
Never.

*

This path, smeared slope through docks, bramble, willow herb,
garden backs going feral, boughs rusted with lichens.
Under a tilted fence, a stump, fungus frilled,
tongues grey and waxy as a cold chicken.

Now a lane, a level,
the sun moving gently on a fleck of wind.
Here is a short halt, a straightening,
the code call of a pigeon.

Go on.

A stone gate into the woods,
moon-pale trunks, roots, a dusk
lit with leaves. You can see
the drop of the valley, the far rise
of the grit hills, pale as metal.
There are far noises, the scrape
or ratchet of a tool, a train's rattle
and bore; and here in the path,
a tree ripped out, root maw
mute with shock, grey and black,
its soil cloyed with moulds.
You would lie in these leaves
if there were time;
sleep into the afternoon.

*

Paths strike out across peat, among ferns,
bog pools. You might know lark's nests,
hare scrapes, the shush of an adder.
There is a hoof-hole full of petrol.

Things go back and back: cows, a fence,
pines at the edge, their poles framing pearl-haze.
You could run at it, bolt the black cattle and leap.
Look though out along these dry rides,
the level going. Quicken.
Here are strollers and striders,
some old and gentle on their feet
or with the grandkids swinging puddles
and whooping
chasing at the cows
the dog

*

Houndkirk Road is scoured to its roots,
torn stones morained against heather stalks:
a way across an emptiness.

Sandstone runs into the hard grit clough
streaking its coarse face with yellow.
A sheep kneels against the bank
cropping it to the marrow.

The old, black, rock-knuckled heather
of Burbage Moor clings to the rise,
its whiff of soot in the warm wind.
Life is buried deep here.

Between a dry green wall and the brown clatter of water
a milepost
Tidſwell – 10
Buxton – 17
   WH
   JF

On the north face just runes and weather.

*

Ringinglow, ring-barrow,
edge and tuck of kept land,
lanes running under banks
and walls, ears cocked at the moor.

Coming up from the town
this is a last place:
everything tends
to absence and elegy:

smoke from a copse,
the red of rowans,
leaves piled along Fulwood Road,
footsteps' ring.

In the fields here
they turn up old tools
jammed with rust
and impossible to date.

Yet duck under the trees
you hear water, the Porter Brook
finding its course through mud
and bark; and as a car crests
the grey hill and disappears
there are starlings churning
the slipstream like gulls.

The lane drops down from the moor line
and here are the sureties of settlement –
cows, thick-walled farms and cottages,
a low house blushed with ivy.
There are child voices here
and if you stop and look back
there is sun in your eyes
and over the valley fields,
thickening the green, making
the walls solid and brown.

Everything flows towards town,
roads and water:
from this last hill it is there,
that glint and shimmer;
but here, still, is birdsong
and cow song and corn-piled barns
and swallows gathering.

Attercliffe to the General Cemetery, midsummer 1842

The body of the Chartist Samuel Holberry was carried from his mother's house to Sheffield Cemetery on midsummer's day.

1.   She is tiny against the men,
         the undertaker with his hat and stick
         grave and gangling.

         There is no drum,
         the river oblivious in its syncopation;
         but the bearers are ready.

         They bend and lift, turn his head
         to the town, its walls and steeples.

Lady's Bridge chapel, a plate by the chancel where you'd drop a coin for safe journey, the water light through the glass pattering the walls; and as you'd rise, road-sweat slipping your palms on the pew, the town ahead – drink and meat, women's faces glimpsed in shadow – would make you, licking flecks of salt from the corners of your mouth, forget your back, knees, the bleeding rawness of your feet.

2.   In the throat of Waingate,
         a bearer stumbles against the crowd.
         The pall droops and steadies.

         As the cortege passes the market-houses,
         the sellers stop their clangour.

Hares and pigeons hang from their sticks
and strings, dark and still:
only the flies weave or waver.

A load of tat laid out over the bright pavement, plastic mostly,
alloy and rubber. Stuff you wouldn't look at in a shop, shining
brilliant though it is. My kids would like it, the colours and
shimmers (and flips and pops and slow unwinding of mechanisms),
but not so much that they couldn't be brought away.

3.   Medieval and narrow High Street
          is choked, blocking the mourners' view
          of the Church of St Peter and St Paul
          as they turn past the shambles
          and the butter market,
          the undertaker bending his back
          to the top of the hill.

Under the green pressing air, buses squeeze together, passengers
gaping for signs of their destinations. You can't hear them, can't
recognise any of them. They go on, staring forwards and outwards,
fists clenched or loosed, mouths slack or fixed or moving, miming
their lives to one another, one word then the next.

4.   They turn into Eyre Lane,
          its workshops full of shades.

          These were his neighbours;
          they have stilled their wheels
          and files for him.

They stand at his passing,
uncapped and silent and grim.

17 to 21 The Pearl Works. The roof is gone, door smashed, glass
chips across the floor. There is light coming through the cavities,
shine on painted door frames and nails for hooks. A vice clings to
a bench, even its brute strength going. The handle is at ten past
eight; or twenty to two.

5.   In an alley near South Lane
        someone has planted flowers
        in drums and pails:
        poppies, daisies, nasturtiums;
        sweet peas, pink and lilac
        against the black brick.

I move beyond the city, the cemetery trees and spires ahead. Here
is Bow Works, a gold clock; horseshoes and bishops' mitres on the
gate. There are plane trees and sycamore trees in the street, skips,
pigeons. In Stalker Lees Road an old man passes along in hat and
mittens like a winter day. Here is the way in, Porter Brook rushing
under, the gates open.

6.   The priest starts,
        his voice high and thin.

        In the trees' shade
        the bearers' faces are dark
        against their white collars.

Now they can see where they came,
the line of people all the way back
to the town. Still they come.

He's in a row, five stones damp and leaning in the bottle-green air.
Briars and nettles, dark holly, deep soil-scent. *For advocating what*
to him appeared to be the true interest of the people of England this
tablet was erected by his bereft widow. A blackbird's shrill clucking.
There must be a cat hereabouts, sniffing after her fledging young,
their beaks open.

Princess Street to the Wicker, April 1925

The journey made by members of the Park Brigade, a notorious gang,
following the murder of a soldier.

There is work going on in the English Pewter Company,
knocking and whirring through the windows, a radio.
On the bridge, green is spouting, nettles and ferns –
there must be rain trapped in the mortar, drip feeding
tap roots, each train's quake slaking the filaments.
The river shudders, ripples like milk skin.

This is where they found mixing chromium with steel
stopped the steel corroding. 1913, all the world mustering
arms, a knife's edge. You could throw it in the river,
it would still be there, flashing in the stones like a fish.
In Princess Street, the arches bricked in, windows blackened,
these last terrace houses are shiftless and feral.

They said the blade that killed Jock Plommer was a bayonet
kept in a black case, elbow to fingertip long. As he sits dying
in his doorway and his wife not touching or looking
at the dark wet pooling on her step, faces come with a light,
with their bits of story, the bottles and razors, the lead
and steel of the Park Brigade men, seven or ten of them.

They hit him on the head with a bottle.
They hit him on the head with a child's scooter.

From the corner you could go anywhere, Leveson Street,
Warren Street, under the arches of Norfolk Bridge, over the river,
its yellow silt, a white duck dabbing in the chiaroscuro.

Here is a tossing ring under the arches, the ha'pennies spinning
over men's heads. In the dusk the pikers watch for the cops.
Whistle as the coins drop, watch them scatter.

In the event of any road vehicle striking this bridge

Between the white van pulling up and the BMW pulling away
there is nothing but the wide, pale urban sweep of Attercliffe Road,
its flat curve featureless as a hinterland. It has outgrown
the river with its births and deaths, its awkward stinks and noises.
In the cool glaze of a showroom, a red Ferrari and a blue Porsche
occupy their exact spaces. Exhilaration, seduction and power

says the sign, vehicles to stir your soul. There's not a soul about.
The Park boys swagger towards town with blood on their hands.
United have just won the FA Cup and the pubs are full of it.
As they come past the gates of Albion Works, their faces
twilit and pale, you can hear their swearing right down Saville Street.
In the gun-green glass of Saville House I am a silhouette, a trace.

You have the right not to remain silent

PC Hogan puts his notebook away, hand pinched from scrawling
names and weapons. The victim is hauled to the ambulance,
people at every door. Lol Fowler, Wilfred Fowler, George Wills,
Amos Stewart: they know the names better than United's eleven.
The road slows into the Wicker arch, its bus-lit shadows.
Here is transience and lycanthropy, somewhere to get lost.

They have put benches here, but no-one settles or waits.
The Station Hotel's the key, Commercial Accommodation,
dinner at the bar, the windows to the street grimy, back rooms

looking at nothing, brick and washing. There are no longer
trains to Manchester, but even the weed strewn line curves away.
A green cross outside the pharmacy flickers, entranced, entropic.

Bottles in bags and in crates, empties.
A substation: *Danger of death*

This was called Bridgehouses, low-rent shanty below the town,
the river turning round it and under it. In flood the water surges
into the street, filling cellar after cellar with black stink.
Nothing is here forever. In The Big Gun, in the Bull and Oak,
no-one flinches, even when a glass is smashed on the bar,
even when a man goes down, face in his bloody fingers.

Between the Bull and the river once, the shambles, raw butchery
with its reek and swill. This is where they got them, the Park gang,
slashing and fighting, blood and spit and snot. The river is hissing
under Lady's Bridge where the road ends and the town begins,
where the castle was and now the market, its pet shop smell
and café fluorescence. Everything must go, the river goes.

Hillsborough to Middlewood, February 1931

The short journey between my great grandparents' house and the South Yorkshire Asylum, where their son Harold died. The Asylum (later known as Middlewood Hospital) has been redeveloped as private housing.

I.M. Harold Hindle, 1904 – 32

Kipling Road

When I come into the street
a woman crosses between parked cars
and hurries away like a straggler.
I stand in her eddy, feeling the air for a way in.

It is a short, stub-ended row of houses,
earth bank at the bottom, the sun on the pavement,
the earliness. There is nothing of sorrow here
except the dead end, its terraced shadow.

Now there is the click of a back door,
the chitter of a budgerigar.
Then you are hurrying from one of these houses,
hair brushed, tangled feet booted,

your undone laces tripping behind you.
I follow.

The Tram Lines

A heron tracks the snow-surged water
even as it's squeezed between factories
and people's gardens, even when the skinhead crows
come taunting and crowding.

But here is water lying on the tram lines,
streets like soaked fields, brown, silver, black.
A tram skirls and squeals on the curve,
soft shadow chasing over the bridge

and onto the bright hill. In the butcher's
a woman feels it brushing by, stutters with her order.
Here, too, the heron would lose its bright thread,
its way in and back. If you saw him close, then,

fumbling his turn, lurching, you might have to run,
you might have to stop thinking.

Green

Everyone is going the wrong way,
toward the post office, the spilled crates
of carrots and rhubarb and stark lemons,
the thick smell of pastry and gravy.

There is an old man bristling and muttering,
a young man with a bag of straw and a bag of apples.
A woman watches her stiff legs moving:
they are too big for her, too young and limber.

The park has been better than now, bright
as it is with litter. Dogs pelt over the empty grass
in front of the library; people move slowly
in the distance. It's a beautiful day, this,

but no-one is sitting still. I wish for some cloud,
some texture on the thin green.

Middlewood Tram Terminus

There are houses still further along, new flats
with crisp squares of gloom and sun,
but this is where the tram stops and the driver
saunters for a smoke. All the doors are open,

thrown tickets flapping like decked fish.
There's a bus in, rattling and twitching, hyper,
names of villages hectic above the windscreen.
This was once my territory, that hill with the GR

post box at the bottom, school at the top,
the park where I rushed along one day, my mind,
gleeful and vicious, running after me. Middlewood,
childhood cant, that thing in all our cellars,

I shouldn't have dared. I pay out my breaths
like twine, each step shortening.

Asylum

Cutting past the old gate house I get it,
the cool of trees, the stillness, a blackbird
fishing the leaf mould for snails: I expect ghosts,
old soldiers, shouts, twitching; I expect singing.

It is changed, though, houses and walkways neat
and empty almost. The architect would call it Haven
I imagine: safe, close to heaven.
It's a nice job, the decorative stone from the halls

cleaned up and flowery, the boarded chapel secured
with thorns and a strong fence. Up at the lodge
where they'd have you signed in, the clock goes on,
the locked front door gleams and the tiny cameras

look at everything. As I leave something clicks, twice:
tut tut. Through your eyes I see myself out.

Dore Moor to the Marples Hotel, 12 December 1940

A descent in the traces of the first of the Luftwaffe raids on Sheffield.

Ecgbert

People lust for this place,
its arrangement of copses and small fields,
hills layering the light into the south.

It is a no man's land: a glamour
between the high emptiness
and a ditch of water.

Dore – an end and a beginning:
King of Wessex and Mercia
come to take oaths from York.

A car pelts past me into Old England,
Ecgbert's broad *scīrs* laid out like a cloth
napped by the tread of his armies' *blitzkrieg*.

The sun sets my shadow in the road north;
I start down into the city,
its roofs pale along the tree-line.

scīrs   OE shires

Whirlow

An incendiary came down in the avenue,
missing the private hospital and the houses,
wrecking the garden walls of Woodglade
and The Lawns, searing the bark from
the old beech, waking the children,
setting devils dancing in the nursery windows.

Ecclesall Woods

This must be a way into the underworld.
The road is straight, with old green iron lamps,
the footpath creped with leaves. I overtake
a man holding himself in his slow, metered walk.
The trees are great, thick things, anchored
in the green gloom. Under huge webs of dead
wood, water moves in its mulched channels.

Further in, the elms hold their hacked limbs
free of brambles. The paths trail uncertainly
into shade, some closed off by nettles or rubble.
The story is of a blast throwing the old earth
right out onto Dobcroft Road. I stand among
the year's dormancy, windows of bathrooms
and back bedrooms dark and unreflective.

Millhouses

A spine, a vessel:
road then slender
tongue of grass
the railway up
on its bed of stones
and staves
the river
its black bank

Bombs along
all this length
trampling houses
here
and here
here

St Oswald

Dusk, the streets close and grey.
On the church door are monks' words.
Matins. Evensong.
Lights of queuing cars bleed the stone
of the church walls, the glow like old fires.

At the end of the road, the clock-eyed school
slumps under its cupola, swept rooms empty
as truants' chairs. Bombs fell crashing
into its silence but spared the church,
its praying faithful, its sinners.

First Siren

The siren has gone on and on, unsettling,
like a baby left to cry who will not sleep.
Still, it stops: just coal, now, dropping to ash.
Just doors shutting. Just the low urgency of voices
next door, upstairs, in the street. Just the clock.
Just footsteps and Mrs Wilkins calling her boys.
Just footsteps. Just a baby crying.

Nether Edge

Allotments terrace the edge,
the climb fenced with privet and old doors.
Light clings here, setting fires in the glass.
The soil beds are mounded with carpets
or left bare for frosts to crack them.

There is nothing here that bombs
would make a difference. All those houses
wrecked, lives spilled into the street
like seeds; but this low-rent fallowland
persists, all ruin and renewal.

From Sharrow Head House

The last lip of the hills trembles:
trees, gables, the cemetery's brown wall
grey in the dusk. In a garden
an empty spire of canes is draped
with bean husks. They chatter.

The skyline has gone. Lights,
flickering from blocks or tracking streets,
make an approximation of the city.
Imagine even these snuffed out,
the ghost-limbed hills, the siren's railing.

Night: Ext

A quiet street in Sheffield. Off right is London Road, busy with
queuing traffic and full of the lights of restaurants, cafes, shop
frontages and pubs. People walk purposefully away from town,
singly or in pairs.

The street cuts between a block of flats and a row of older brick
buildings: a works office, a repair shop, a Baptist church. A man
comes into the street. He is wearing a trench coat, open and
swinging. He passes down.

Ahead is the subway with its yellow light. It is empty except for a
small dark mass, too small to be anyone, against the green tiled wall
left. From this distance it might be a bag or dog or jacket.

Above is the ring road which by its noise is thick with traffic.
Only tops of trucks and buses are visible from the street which is
lower and shielded by metal barriers and a concrete balustrade.
Above the ring road are the high office blocks. Some windows
are lit; most not.

It is very cold and though the light bleeds up into the sky for miles,
still from this quiet street, directly above is a small strip of deep blue
which the light has made black; and looking carefully reveals three
stars from the constellation of Cassiopeia, tiny fragments.

Two boys come along a path that runs round the flats. One is
on a small bike, the other on foot. They stop and look at the
entrance to the flats for some seconds, then head off across a
patch of ground towards the colour of London Road – the cyclist
walking his bike.

A girl comes out of the subway, passing the still dark shape. She is speaking into her mobile phone and doesn't notice the form. As she leaves the lit tunnel her clothes change from white and green to orange and grey, her hair from red to black.

'Man he's just proper dead.'

Marples

The Marples Hotel took a direct hit at 10:58pm. Over seventy people, sheltering in the cellars, were killed. Seven men survived, two of them walking away into the night.

The city burns like an effigy.

Lit smoke in the belly of the cathedral, its back end gone.
You can't get down High Street, you should go home.

I was on the tram, two women
– I lost me Nan
– Oh Christine

Stained glass exploding into Campo Lane,
corn from a slashed sack.

Kings Head, the Angel, the Bodega.
Shades Vaults on Watson's Walk.
Mains water frothing into Angel Street
looking for the river.

A couple, her holding his arm
– Alright here, Frank?
gripping it, steering
– Frank. Here?

Tram tracks sprung from the road like roots.
The tram at West Bar, decks ripped apart,
seats strewn and mangled.

Cockayne's the drapers on Angel Street.
John Walsh's stores round the corner on High Street.
F G Thomas, heraldic stationers.
H L Brown the jewellers.
Syminton and Croft's; the Co-op City Stores;
C & A Modes, white as a wedding.
– It come down like a pack of cards.

Everywhere the smoke
like ink in water
everywhere fires like marsh gas.

Buildings stagger, some jawed open over the street.
In among the ghost shapes, firemen creep on ladders,
on roofs, black figures small against the great dead bulk:
the Central Picture House; John Shaw's works; the theatre;
the furniture shop: all hollow, brittle, a carapace.

They put special shows on down in the vaults,
white faces, smoke drifting out of the light.
A thump, everything jolts, shivers.
Bits of plaster on the tables, in the beer.
The band picks up, faces turn to each other again.

Out of the city is a moon world, blue and white,
frost like gas on the fields and roads.
The land slips east into night, fen ditches
glowing like pig-iron. High in the thin air
the planes drum towards the coast.

– *Touch wood Christine. Touch some wood.*

Geese crowd the Wash, silver flats
full of their clamouring. Shadows ripple
over them, rows of crosses, another,
another.

Notes

Death and the Gallant Chris Jones
The extract of *The Journal of William Dowsing* I use here comes from a
volume edited by the Rev C. H. Evelyn White (published in 1885). A
full copy of Dowsing's text can be read online in various versions. My
interest in Pre-Reformation wall painting came in part from Andrew
Graham-Dixon's television series *A History of British Art* and his
accompanying book (1996). The first chapter, 'Dreams and Hammers',
offers an excellent introduction to ideas of iconoclasm and its effects
on the British psyche. For a more academic overview of iconoclasm
during the Reformation, see Eamon Duffy's *The Stripping of the Altars*
(Yale University Press, 2005). Much of the information I use for *Death
and the Gallant* comes from *Medieval Wall Paintings* by Roger Rosewell
(The Boydell Press, 2008). Finally, an online resource I frequently
visited was Paintedchurch.org. The site catalogues many examples of
various Biblical (and religious) paintings, offering glimpses of how our
medieval churches would have appeared to their congregations.

From _From a St Juliot to Beyond a Beeny_ Mark Goodwin
OS Explorer Map 111: Bude, Boscastle & Tintagel is recommended for
useful & aesthetic accompaniment. In August 2004 the River Valency
(*Dowr an Velinji* in Cornish) flooded, causing extensive damage to
the harbour village of Boscastle. It has been suggested that the name
Valency is a corruption of the Cornish *Melinjy*, or *Melin-Chy*, which
means mill-house, possibly referring to the mill in medieval times.
The poem is full of 'corrupted' names. This extract from *From a St
Juliot to Beyond a Beeny* is abstracted and reworked (or 're-mapped')
from a much longer poem in the forthcoming collection *Steps*
(Longbarrow Press, 2014). The version in *The Footing* has been edited
creatively in collaboration with Brian Lewis.

Flights and Traverses Rob Hindle
The main source for 'Princess Street to the Wicker' was *The Sheffield
Gang Wars* by J P Bean (D & D Publications, 1981). The Picture
Sheffield website (www.picturesheffield.com), maintained by Sheffield
Archives and Local Studies Service, was a valuable source of inspiration
for the 'Marples' section of 'Dore Moor to the Marples Hotel'.